Word

English Readers

Lee and Pat go with Daddy

Story and Pictures by Philip Gibson

Hello.

Look.
Look here.
Look at this book.

Lee and Pat are here.
They are here with Kim.
Lee and Pat like Kim.

I like Kim, too.
Kim is a good dog.
He likes to play.

He likes to play with Lee
and Pat.

Look.
Look at this book.
Look at Kim.
Look at Lee.
Look at Pat, too.

New Word: **does**

Here is Lee. Lee has a ball.
Lee likes the ball. He likes
to play with the ball.

The ball is not big. It is
small. It is a small ball.

Lee likes to play with the
ball and Pat does, too.

Is Lee here?
        Yes, he is.

Is the ball here?
        Yes, it is.

Does Lee like the ball?
        Yes, he does.

Does Pat like the ball.
        Yes, she does.

Here is Kim. He is with a ball, too. He likes to play with this ball. It is good. It is a good ball. This ball is big. Kim likes to play with it and Lee does, too.

Kim likes to play with this ball. He likes to play with Lee and Pat. He likes to play with Lee, Pat and the ball. They like to play with the ball. It is good to play with this ball.

1. Is the ball here?
   Yes, it ____.

2. Does Lee like to play?
   Yes, he ____.

3. Does Pat like the ball?
   Yes, she ____.

4. Is the ball big?
   Yes, it ____.

3

New Word: **house**

Here is a house. Look at
the house. It is not small.
It is big. It is a big house. It
is good. It is a good house.
Lee likes the house. Pat
does too. Lee and Pat like
the big house.

Lee is with Pat. He is with Pat and Kim. Lee
looks at the house. Pat looks at the house. Kim,
the dog, does too. Kim looks at the house with
Lee and Pat.

Is the house small?

     No, it is not.

Is it big?

     Yes, it is.

Does Lee like the house?

     Yes, he does.

Does Pat like the house?

     Yes, she does.

What is this?

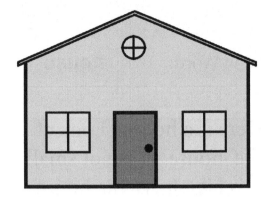

This is a house, too. Look at this house. This house is not big. This house is small. It is a small house.

Lee and Pat like this house, too. They like the big house and they like the small house. Lee and Pat like the small house and Kim does, too. Kim, the dog, likes the small house and the big house.

    1. Does Lee like the big house?
        Yes, he ____.

    2. Does he like the small house?
        Yes, ____ does.

    3. Is Lee with Kim?
        Yes, he ____.

    4. Is Pat here, too?
        Yes, ____ is.

New Word: **cat**

Look. Here is a cat. This cat is not big. It is small. It is a small cat.

The cat looks at the house. It looks at the house with Pat. Pat likes this cat, and the cat likes Pat. The cat likes to play. It likes to play with the ball. It likes to play with Pat, too.

Is the cat big?
            No, it is not.
Is it small?
            Yes, it is.

Does Pat like the cat?
            Yes, she does.

Does the cat like to play?
            Yes, it does.

Here is Lee. Lee likes Pat. He likes the house, and he likes to play. He likes to play with Kim, the dog. He does not like to play with the cat.

Lee does not like the cat. Lee does not like the cat, and the cat does not like Lee. Lee likes the dog. The dog likes Lee. Pat likes the cat. Lee does not.

1. Is Lee here?
   _____, he is.

2. Does he like the house?
   Yes, he _____.

3. Does he like the cat?
   _____, he does not.

4. Does he like the dog?
   _____, he does.

New Word: **that**

Pat likes the cat. Lee does not. Lee does not like the cat. Lee likes the dog. He does not like that cat.

*This cat is good.
I like this cat.*

No. That cat is not good. The dog is good. That cat is not good.

Is the cat with Lee?
No, it is not.
Is it with Pat?
Yes, it is.

Does Lee like that cat?
No, he does not.

Does Pat like it?
Yes, she does.

Lee. Look.
Look at that house.
It is big. I like that house.

Yes, that is a big house. I like it, too. I like that house. I like Kim. I like the ball. I like ice-creams. I like bananas. I like oranges. I like books, too. They are good. That cat is not good!

1. Is Pat here?
    Yes, ____ ____.

2. Is Lee here?
    Yes, ____ ____.

3. Does Lee like that house?
    Yes, ____ ____.

4. Does he like the cat?
    No, ____ ____ ____.

New Word: **in**

Look at that cat.

What cat?

That cat. Look.
That cat is in the house.
That is not good.
That cat is not good.

Yes, it is. That cat is good. It
is a good cat. I like that cat.

Is the cat in the house?
Yes, it is.

Is the dog in the house?
No, it is not.

Is Lee here?
Yes, he is.

Is Pat here?
Yes, Pat is here, too.

Look here. Pat is in the house. She is with the cat. Pat likes to play with that cat. She likes to play with the cat in the house. The cat likes it, too. The cat likes to play in the house.

Lee is not in the house. Lee does not like that cat. He likes the dog. He likes Kim. He likes to play with Kim. He does not like to play with the cat. Lee does not like cats.

1. Is Pat in the house?

    ____, ____ ____.

2. Is Lee in the house?

    ____, ____ ____ ____.

3. Does the cat like to play in the house?

    ____, ____ ____.

4. Does Lee like to play with the cat?

    ____, ____ ____ ____.

New Word: **you**

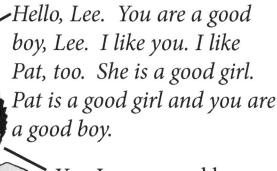

Hello, Lee. You are a good boy, Lee. I like you. I like Pat, too. She is a good girl. Pat is a good girl and you are a good boy.

Yes, I am a good boy. I am good. Pat is good. Kim is good. The cat is not good.

Is Lee a good boy?
    Yes, he is.

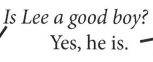

Is Pat a good girl?
    Yes, she is. She is a good girl.

Is Kim good?
    Yes, he is. He is a good dog.

Are you good?
    Yes, I am. I am good, too.

Hello, Pat. You are a good girl, Pat. You are good and Lee is good, too. I like you and Lee.

What is that?

This is a cat. I like this cat. I like to play with this cat. It is a good cat. I like it. Lee does not like it. Lee does not like cats.

1. Is Pat here?

   ____, ____ ____.

2. Does Lee like the cat?

   ____, ____ ____ ____.

3. Is Pat good?

   ____, ____ ____.

4. Are you good?

   ____, ____ ____.

8

New Word: **garden**

Look here. What is this? This is a garden. Lee and Pat are here. They are here in the garden. They are here in the garden with Kim, the dog. They like to play in the garden with Kim.

The cat is not in the garden. The cat is in the house. The cat likes to play in the house. It likes to play in the garden, too. It does not play with Lee and Pat in the garden. Lee does not like the cat.

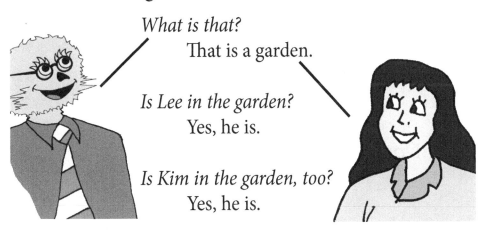

What is that?
    That is a garden.

Is Lee in the garden?
    Yes, he is.

Is Kim in the garden, too?
    Yes, he is.

Is the cat in the garden?
    No, it is not.

Hello, Kim. You are a good dog, Kim. You like Lee. You like Pat, too. You like to play. You like to play with Lee and Pat. You like to play in the garden. You are a good dog. I like you.

1. Is Kim here?

    ———, ——— ———.

2. Does he like Lee and Pat?

    ———, ——— ———.

3. Does he like to play?

    ———, ——— ——— ———.

4. Is he a good dog?

    ———, ——— ———.

New Word: **or**

Is this Lee or Pat?

This is Pat.

Is she in the garden or in the house?

She is in the garden.

And Lee? Is he in the garden or in the house?

Lee is in the house with Kim.

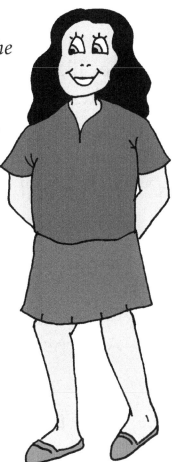

Kim? Is Kim a dog or a cat?

Kim is a dog.

Does Kim like Lee or Pat?

Kim likes Lee and Pat.

Does Lee like the cat or the dog?

Lee likes the dog.
He does not like the cat.

Look here. Is this Lee or Pat? This is Lee. Look at Lee. Lee has a ball. Is it big or small? It is big. Lee likes to play with that big ball. Does he like to play with it in the garden or in the house? He likes to play with it in the garden.

Is Lee with the dog or the cat? He is with the dog. Lee likes the dog and he likes to play with it. He likes to play with it in the garden. He does not like to play with the cat. Lee does not like cats.

1. Is the ball big or small?

    ____ ____ ____.

2. Is Lee with the cat or the dog?

    ____ ____ ____ ____ ____.

3. Are they in the house or the garden?

    ____ ____ ____ ____ ____.

4. Does Lee like the cat or the dog?

    ____ ____ ____ ____.

18

New Word: **happy**

Look at Pat. Pat is in the house. She is in the house with the cat. Pat likes that cat. That cat likes Pat. Pat is happy. The cat is happy, too. Pat has the ball. Pat and the cat play with the ball. Pat and the cat are happy.

Is Pat in the garden?
> No, she is not. She is in the house.

Is she with the cat or the dog?
> She is with the cat.

Is she happy?
> Yes, she is.

And Lee? Is Lee happy?
> No he is not. Lee is not happy.

Look at Lee. Lee is not happy. Lee does not like the cat. He does not like the cat to play with Pat. He does not like the cat to play with the ball. He does not like the cat
to play in the house.
He is not happy.
Pat is happy.
Lee is not.

1. Is Lee happy?

_____, _____ _____ _____.

2. Does he like the cat to play with Pat?

_____, _____ _____ _____.

3. Does he like it to play in the house?

_____, _____ _____ _____.

4. Is Pat happy?

_____, _____ _____.

New Words: **very**
want

You are not good Pat.

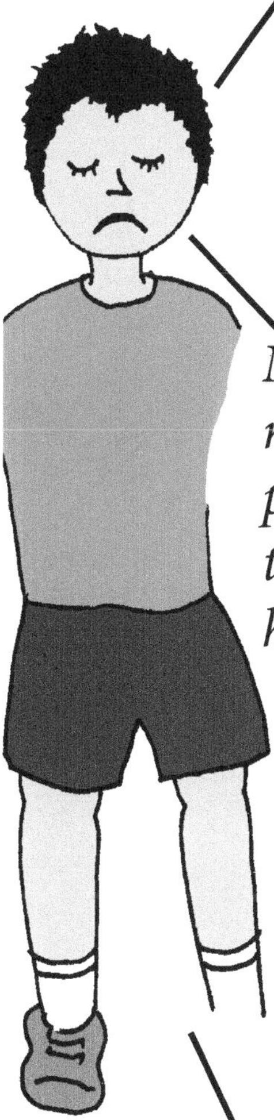

Yes, I am.
I am a good
girl. I am a
very good girl.

*No, you are not. You are
not a good girl. You like to
play with the cat. You like
to play with the cat in the
house. That is not good.*

It is good. It is
good to play
with the cat. The
cat is good. The
cat is very good.
The cat is happy.
It is very happy.
I am happy, too.

You are happy, Pat. I am not.

Look here. What is this? This is a garden. Lee and Pat are here. They are here in the garden. They are here in the garden with Kim, the dog. They like to play in the garden with Kim.

1. Are Lee and Pat here?

    ———, ——— ———.

2. Are they happy?

    ———, ——— ——— ———.

3. Does Lee want to play with Pat?

    ———, ——— ——— ———.

4. And Pat? Does Pat want to play with Lee?

    ———, ——— ——— ———.

New Words: **fun**
Where....?

Where is the dog? The dog is in the garden. Look at the dog. The dog has fun with the ball. It likes to play with the ball in the garden. It is fun. The cat is not here. The cat does not want to play with the dog. The cat does not like the dog.

Where is the dog?
　　The dog is in the garden.

Where is the cat?
　　The cat is in the house.

Where are Lee and Pat?
　　They are in the house, too.

Are they happy?
　　No, they are not. Lee and Pat
　　are not very happy.

23

Where is Pat? Pat is in the house. She is not with Lee. Pat is not happy with Lee. Pat has a book. She likes to look at that book. It is fun. That book is very good. It is a very good book. Pat likes to look at books.

Lee does not want to look at books. Lee likes to play with the dog. Lee has fun with the dog. Lee wants to play with the dog. It is fun.

1. Where is Pat?

   _____.

2. Is Lee with Pat?

   _____.

3. Does Pat like to look at that book?

   _____.

4. Is it fun?

   _____.

New Words: **tree**
                      go
                      it's

Look at the cat. Where is it? Where is the cat? The cat is in a tree. That cat likes to go in trees. It likes to go in that tree. It likes to play in that tree. It is fun.

Kim, the dog, is not in the tree. Kim does not like to go in trees. He does not want to go in that tree. That tree is very big.

Where is the cat?
    It is in the tree.

Is it a big tree?
    Yes. It's very big.

Where is the tree?
    It's in the garden.

Does Kim like to go in trees?
No, he does not.

Look. Here is Kim. Kim is with the cat. Kim and the cat are in the garden. Kim is not happy. Kim does not like the cat. The cat is not happy. The cat does not like the dog. Lee and Pat are not here. They are in the house.

1. Is the dog in the house or in the garden?

    _____.

2. Is the dog happy?

    _____.

3. Does the dog play with the cat?

    _____.

4. Where are Lee and Pat?

    _____.

New Word: **does**

The cat can go in the tree. That tree is very big.
The dog can not go in the tree. The dog does not
 want to go in trees. The
dog likes to go in the
garden, and it likes to
go in the house. It is
fun to go in the garden.
It is fun to go in the
house. The dog does
not want to go in trees.
It can not go in trees.

Is the cat in the garden or the house?
It is in the garden.

Can the cat go in the tree?
Yes, it can.

Can the dog go in the tree?
No, it can not.

Is it fun in the garden?
Yes, it is.

Look. Lee is with the cat. The cat is not very happy. The cat can not go in the house. The dog can go in the house. The cat can not. Lee does not want the cat to go in the house.

You are not good. You are not a good cat. You can not go in the house. The dog can go in the house. You can not go in the house!

1. Is Lee with the cat?

   _____.

2. Can the cat go in the house?

   _____.

3. Can the dog go in the house?

   _____.

4. Is the cat happy?

   _____.

15

New Words: **water**
               over there

Look. Look over there. Lee is over there. He is over there with Kim. Kim is in the water. Kim likes to go in the water. It is fun to go in the water.

The cat is not over there. The cat does not like to go in the water. The cat does not want to go in the water.

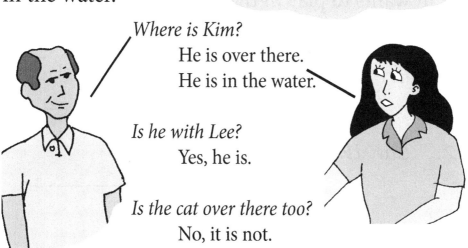

Where is Kim?
> He is over there.
> He is in the water.

Is he with Lee?
> Yes, he is.

Is the cat over there too?
> No, it is not.

Where is the cat?
> The cat is in the house with Pat.

Look over there. Pat is over there with the cat. Pat likes to play with the cat. It is fun to play with the cat. The cat can go in trees. The cat likes to play in trees.

The dog is not over there. The dog is with Lee. It is in the water. The dog likes to go in the water. It does not want to go in trees. It does not want to play with the cat. It wants to play in the water with Lee.

1. Is Pat with the cat?

   _____.

2. Can the cat go in trees?

   _____.

3. Is the dog over there?

   _____.

4. Where is the dog?

   _____.

New Words: **Lee's dog**
               Pat's cat

Look over there. That is Pat's cat.
Pat likes that cat. She likes to play
with the cat in the garden. It is fun.
It is fun to play with the cat.
Pat's cat is good. Pat's cat is
a good cat. It likes to play.
It likes to play in the garden.
It likes to play in the tree.
It does not like to play in water.
Pat's cat does not like water.

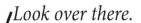

Look over there.

Where?

Over there. Look.
Look at Pat's cat.

Yes. Pat's cat is over
there. It is in the tree.

Yes. Pat is over there, too.
Pat is over there with the cat.
Pat likes to play with that cat.

Look over there. That is Kim.
Kim is Lee's dog. Lee's dog
is good. Lee's dog is very
good. Lee's dog can play.
Lee's dog can play with the
ball. It can play with Lee,
too. Lee's dog can play in the
garden. It can play in the house, too. Lee likes the
dog to play in the house.

Lee does not want the cat to go in the house. Lee
does not like that cat. Lee's dog can play in water.
Pat's cat can not play in water. Pat's cat does not
like to go in water.

1. Is that Lee's dog?

    _____.

2. Is Lee's dog good?

    _____.

3. Can Lee's dog go in water?

    _____.

4. Can Pat's cat go in water?

    _____.

New Word: **do**

Look here. Look at Pat's cat. Pat's cat wants to go in the house. It wants to go play in the house.

Pat wants the cat to go in the house. She wants it to go in and play.

Lee does not. Lee does not want the cat to go in the house. Pat is not happy.

Is Pat's cat here?
    Yes, it is.

Can it go in the house?
    No, it can not.

Is Pat in the house or in the garden?
    Pat is in the house.

Is Pat's cat happy?
    No, it is not. It is not happy.

Lee, the cat wants to go in the house.

The cat can not go in the house. I do not want the cat to go in the house.

I do. I want to play with the cat in the house. It is fun.

No, it is not. The cat is not good. That cat can not go in the house. The dog can go in the house. That cat can not. I do not like that cat.

1. Is the cat in the house?

   _____.

2. Does the cat want to go in the house?

   _____.

3. Can it go in the house?

   _____.

4. Can the dog go in the house?

   _____.

New Words: **Daddy**
            car

Look. Here is Daddy. He is Lee's Daddy. He is Pat's Daddy, too.

Look over there. Daddy has a car. Look at the car. It is good. It is very good. It is not small. It is big. It is very big. It is a very big car.

Daddy likes that car. He likes to go in the car with Lee and Pat. Lee and Pat likes the car, too. They want to go in the car.

Do you like Daddy's car?
    Yes, I do.

Does Daddy like it?
    Yes, he does.

Is Daddy's car big?
    Yes, it is. It is very big.

Can you go in the car?
    Yes, I can. I can go with Daddy.

Do you like Daddy's car?

Yes, I do. It's a very good car. I want to go in Daddy's car.

1. Does Pat like Daddy's car?

   _____.

2. What does she want to do?

   _____.

3. Do you like the car?

   _____.

4. Do you want to go in it?

   _____.

New Words: **come**
             me
             don't

Hello, Daddy. Daddy,
can I go with you?
Can I go with
you in the car?

Yes, Lee. You are a good
boy. You can come. You
can come in the car
with me.

Where is the car, Daddy?

It is over there. Look.
Look over there. The
car is over there.
Do you like it? Do you like the car?

Yes, I do. It's a very good car. It is not
small. It's very big. I like big cars.
I don't like small cars. I like big cars.

What do Lee and Pat want to do? They want to go with Daddy. They want to go with Daddy in Daddy's car. Daddy's car is very good. It is not small. It is big. It is very big. Lee and Pat like Daddy's car. The dog and the cat like it, too. Lee, Pat, the dog and the cat all want to go in the car. They all want to go in Daddy's car.

Look at the cat and the dog. They want to go in the car, too. They want to go in the car with Lee and Pat. Can they? Can the dog and the cat go in the car? Can they go with Daddy, Lee and Pat?

1. What do Lee and Pat want to do?

    _____.

2. Do they want to go with Daddy?

    _____.

3. Is the car big?

    _____.

4. What do the cat and the dog want to do?

    _____.

New Words: **Mommy**
cannot

Look. Look here.
Mommy is here.
This is Pat's mommy.
She is Lee's mommy, too.

Is Mommy here?
　　Yes, she is. Lee, Kim
　　and I are here, too.

Where is the cat?
　　The cat is not here.
　　The cat cannot come
　　in the house.

Do you like the cat?
　　Yes, I do. It's a good cat.

Do you want it to come in the house?
　　Yes, I do. Can it, Daddy? Can it
　　come in the house?

Look at the cat and the dog. The cat wants to go in the house. The cat cannot go in the house. The dog does not want the cat to go in the house. The dog does not like the cat. The cat does not like the dog. The cat and the dog are not happy.

1. What does the cat want to do?

   _____.

2. Can the cat go in the house?

   _____.

3. Does the dog want the cat to go in the house?

   _____.

4. Are the dog and cat happy?

   _____.

New Word: **children**

Look at the children. The children are here with Kim and the cat. The children want to go with Daddy. They want to go with Daddy in Daddy's car. They want Mommy to come, too.

Lee wants Mommy to come. He wants Kim to come. He does not want the cat to come. Pat wants the cat to come. Lee does not.

Hello, Daddy.

Hello, Pat.

Daddy, can I go in the car with you?

Yes, Pat. You are a good girl. You can come in the car with me. Lee can come with me, too.

41

Can the cat come, too?

Yes, the cat can come with me, too. You can come with me. Mommy can come with me. Lee can come with me. The cat can come with me and the dog can come with me, too.

Daddy?

Yes, Pat?

The cat does not like the dog!

1. Can the children go in the car?

    _____.

2. Can the cat come, too?

    _____.

3. And Lee?

    _____.

4. Does the cat like the dog?

    _____.

New Words: **we**
             all

Children, come here. Lee, come here. Pat, come here. Look. We can all go over there. We can all go over there in the car.

You can all come with me.
Lee can come with me.
Pat can come with me.
Mommy can come with me, too.

We can all go. We can all go over there. We can all go over there in the car.

43

Where can the children go? They can go over there. They can go over there in the car. Lee can go. Pat can go. The dog can go. The cat can go. Mommy can go, too. They can all go with Daddy.

Mommy is happy. Daddy is happy, too. The children are not happy. Lee does not want the cat to come. Pat is not happy with Lee. She likes that cat, and she wants it to come, too.

The cat is not happy. The cat wants to go. It wants to go over there in the car with the children.

1.   Where can the children go?

_____.

2.   What can they go in?

_____.

3.   Is Pat happy?

_____.

4.   Where does the cat want to go?

_____.

New Words: **Let's**
Come on!

Come on, Mommy! Let's go.
Let go over there. You can
come with me. We can all go.
We can all go over there.

Yes. Let's go!
Let's go over there.
Let's go over there
in the car.
Come on, children.
Let's go! Pat, let's go!
Lee, let's go!

Mommy, I don't want to go.
It is not fun. It's not fun to go
with the cat. I don't want the
cat to come in the car
with me. I don't want the cat
to go. Mommy, I am not
happy. I don't like that cat.

Daddy wants the children to come in the car. He wants Mommy to come, too. He wants to go. He wants to go over there.

Lee does not want to go. Lee is not happy. He is not a happy boy. He does not want to go in the car with the cat.

Pat wants to go. She wants the cat to come, too. She wants the cat to come in the car. She wants to go. She wants to go over there with Mommy, Daddy, Lee, Kim and the cat.

1. Does Daddy want the children to come?

   _____.

2. Where does he want to go?

   _____.

3. Is Lee happy?

   _____.

4. Does Pat want the cat to come, too?

   _____.

New Words: **have**
Be / be

Come on, Lee! Let's go! Let's go over there. We can have fun over there. It's good. They have trees over there. They have apples, oranges and bananas.

No. I don't want to go. I don't want to go with Pat's cat. Pat's cat is not good. I don't like it. I don't want to go in the car with that cat!

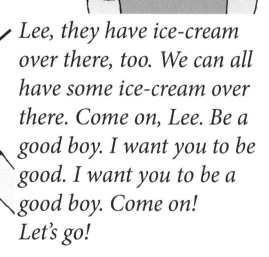

Lee, they have ice-cream over there, too. We can all have some ice-cream over there. Come on, Lee. Be a good boy. I want you to be good. I want you to be a good boy. Come on! Let's go!

Mommy wants Lee to be a good boy. She wants Lee to come in the car. She wants Lee to come in the car with Daddy and Pat. She wants the children to go over there and have ice-cream.

 Mommy is not happy. She wants to go. She wants to go over there. She wants to go with the children. It is good over there. It is fun.

Over there, they can have apples, oranges and bananas. They can have ice-creams, too. Pat and Mommy want to go have ice-cream.

1. Does Mommy want Lee to be a good boy?

    _____.

2. Where does Pat want to go?

    _____.

3. Is it good over there?

    _____.

4. Do they have ice-cream over there?

    _____.

48

New Words: **Please**
us

Daddy, I don't want to go. I don't want to go with that cat. That cat is not good. I don't like it.

Come on, Lee. Please. Please be a good boy. Come in the car with us. Come over there with us. You can be with Kim. The cat can be with Pat.

No, I don't want to. It's not fun. It's not fun to be with the cat. I don't like it.

Come on, Lee. Please. Come with us. It's good over there. It's very good. They have apple trees. They have orange trees. They have bananas and they have ice-creams, too. You like ice-creams. You can have an ice-cream over there. The ice-creams over there are very good. They are not small. They are very big.

49

 *Very big?*

Yes. Very big. Very, very big.
Come on, Lee. Be a good boy.
Come with us. Come with us.
We can go all over there and have ice-cream.

 *Very big ice-creams? Can we have very big ice-creams. Can I have a big ice-cream?*

Yes. Yes, you can. We can all have very big ice-creams.

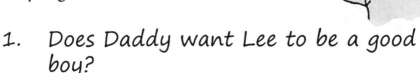

1. Does Daddy want Lee to be a good boy?

    _____.

2. Do they have orange trees over there?

    _____.

3. Are the ice-creams big?

    _____.

4. Can Lee have a big ice-cream?

    _____.

New Word: **see**

Come on, Daddy. Let's go! Can
we go, please?

Go where?
Where do you want to go?

Over there. Let's go. Let's go over
there. Please, Daddy. Please.
Let's go!

What do you want to do over there?

I want to go and see what they have.
I want to see the apple trees. I want to
see the orange trees. I want to see the
banana trees, too.

And ice-creams? Do you want
to see the ice-creams, too?

Yes! Yes! Yes! I want to see the
ice-creams, too. I want to have an
ice-cream. I want to have a big
ice-cream - a very big ice-cream.

Look. Can you see the children?
The children are in Daddy's car.
They are in the car with Mommy
and Daddy. The children
are happy. They are
very happy.

Kim and the cat are happy. Mommy and Daddy
are happy, too. They like the children to be happy.
They want Kim and the cat to be happy, too.

The children want to see what is over there. Pat
wants to see the trees. Lee wants to go have an
ice-cream. He wants to have a very big ice-cream!

1. Where are the children?

    _____.

2. Are they happy?

    _____.

3. What does Pat want to see?

    _____.

4. What does Lee want to do?

    _____.

Look at this. Can you see the trees?
Can you see the oranges and apples?
Can you see the bananas?

Look at Lee.
What can Lee see?

ice - creams

This garden is very good.
I like it. It's fun here. All
the trees are good. The
orange trees are good.
The apple trees are good.
The banana trees are
good, too.

Daddy, I want to go over there. Let's go over there.
Let's see what they have over there. Can we go
over there, please? Please, Daddy. Can we go over
there?

1. Is it fun in the garden?

    _____.

2. Does Lee like it?

    _____.

3. Are the trees good?

    _____.

4. Where does Lee want to go?

    _____.

28

Hello.

Hello.

We like this garden. It's very good.

I am happy you like it. I like it, too. I have a house here. Look. It's over there.

Yes, I can see it. It's very good. We are here with Mommy and Daddy. Kim and the cat are with us, too.

Where are they?

They are over there. They want to look at the trees. Do you have ice-creams in your house?

Yes, we do. Do you want to see? Come on. Let's go and see.

Mommy and Daddy like this garden. They want to see all the trees. Lee does not want to look at the trees. He wants to have an ice-cream.

Mommy and Daddy want the children to have fun here. They want the cat and dog to have fun, too. They want the children to be good. They don't want the children to play in the trees. They don't want the children to play in the water. They want the children to be good. They want the cat and dog to be good, too.

1. Do Mommy and Daddy like the garden?

    _____.

2. What do they want to see?

    _____.

3. Does Lee want to look at the trees?

    _____.

4. What does Lee want to do?

    _____.

29

Here we are, Lee. Here are the ice-creams.
Do you want a small ice-cream or a big ice-cream?

A big ice-cream, please...
...a very big ice-cream.
I like big ice-creams.

And Pat? Does she want an
ice-cream, too?

No, she doesn't. Pat wants to
have an apple or an orange.

Pat can have what she wants.
What does she want? Does she
want an apple or an orange?

An orange, please.
Pat likes oranges.

Does she want a big orange
or a small orange?

A small orange, please.
Pat likes small oranges.

Can you see the children? Look at the children. They are happy. They are very happy. Lee is happy. Lee has an ice-cream. It is big. It is very big. Lee likes big ice-creams.

Can you see Pat? Pat is happy, too. She has an orange. It is a small orange. Pat likes small oranges. Small oranges are good. Mummy and Daddy are happy, too. They want the children to have fun here. They want the children to be happy.

1. Are the children happy?

   _____.

2. What does Lee have?

   _____.

3. And Pat? What does Pat have?

   _____.

4. Is the orange big?

   _____.

Word by Word
English Readers

Book 4

Lee and Pat go to school

We like school!

Story and Pictures by Philip Gibson

New Words: **his**
name

Look at this boy. This is Lee. His name is Lee. Lee is in the garden. He is in the garden with a girl. Lee has a ball. He can play with his ball and this girl in the garden.

This girl is Pat. Lee is playing with Pat. He likes to play with Pat. Lee can play with Pat in the garden. He likes to do that. It's fun.

Pat likes to play in the garden, too. She likes to play in the garden with Lee. She likes to have fun in the garden. It is fun to play in the garden with Lee and his ball.

Daddy
Where is Lee?

Mommy
He is over there. Look! There he is.

Daddy
Yes. Yes, he is. I can see Lee. He is over there with Pat.

Mommy

Yes. Lee and Pat are playing over there, in the garden.

Daddy

Where is Lee's dog? Is his dog in the garden, too?

Mommy

Yes, it is. Lee's dog is over there, too.

Daddy

What is his dog's name?

Mommy

His dog's name is Kim.

Daddy

Is Kim a good dog?

Mommy

Yes, he is. He is a very good dog.

Look at this girl. This girl's name is Pat. Pat is in the garden with Lee and Kim. Kim is Lee's dog. Lee likes his dog. He likes to play in the garden with his dog. Lee, Kim and Pat are playing with Lee's ball.

Lee, Kim and Pat are playing with Lee's small ball. Lee likes his ball. Pat and the dog like his ball, too. It is fun to play with this ball. The children can play with Lee's ball in the garden. It is fun.

The dog wants to play with the ball, too. That ball is not very big. It is a small ball. Lee likes to play with his small ball. Lee, Pat and Kim all like to play with this small ball.

1. *Where is the girl?*
2. *What is the girl's name?*
3. *Is it fun to play in the garden?*
4. *Does the dog want to play with the ball?*
5. *Do the children like the ball?*

64

New Words: **(at) home**
sit (down) / sitting (down)

Here is Lee. Lee is with Pat.
They are in the house.
They are at home.
The children are
sitting down.
Lee is sitting
with Pat. Pat is
sitting with Lee.

Lee has a dog. The dog's name is Kim. Lee likes
his dog. Lee likes all dogs. He likes all dogs, but
he does not like cats. Pat likes cats. Lee does not.

Kim the dog is at home too. Kim is at home with
the children. Lee, Pat and Kim are all at home.
They are all in the house.

Teacher
Is Lee here?

Mommy
Yes, he is.

Teacher
Is he sitting with Pat?

Mommy
Yes, he is.

Teacher
Where are they? Are they in the garden?

Mommy
No, they are not. They are in the house. They are at home.

Teacher
Does Lee have a dog?

Mommy
Yes, he does.

Teacher
What is his dog's name?

Mommy
His dog's name is Kim.

Teacher
Where is Kim?

Mommy
Kim is in the house. He is sitting with Lee and Pat in the house.

This is Kim's dog. The dog's name is Kim. His name is Kim. Lee likes his dog. Kim is a very good dog. Lee likes good dogs. He does not like cats. Lee likes his dog and he likes to play with it. It is fun to play with Kim the dog.

Lee does not like to play with cats. Lee does not like cats. Lee likes to sit with his dog in the house, and he likes to play with his dog in the garden. He likes to play with his dog in the house, too.

1. *What is the dog's name?*
2. *Does Lee like his dog?*
3. *Is Kim a good dog?*
4. *Is Lee sitting with his dog?*
5. *Does Lee like to play with cats?*

New Words: **brother**
               sister
               red

Look at Lee. Can you see Lee? He is not in the garden. He is in the house. He is at home. He is at home with his sister. He is at home with Pat.

Pat is Lee's sister. Lee likes his sister. He likes to play with his sister. Lee can play with his sister in the house. He can play with his sister in the garden, too. Lee likes to do that. It is fun.

Lee is Pat's brother. Pat likes Lee. She likes to play with Lee in the house, and she likes to play with Lee in the garden, too.

Teacher 2
Where is Lee's sister? Is she here?

Teacher 1
No, she isn't. She is not here.

Teacher 2
Where is she?

Teacher 1
She is at home.

Teacher 2
Is she with Daddy?

Teacher 1
No she isn't. She is with Lee.

Teacher 2
Is the dog in the house, too?

Teacher 1
No, it isn't.

Teacher 2
Where is the dog?

Teacher 1
It's in the garden. The dog is in the garden.

Let's go and see Lee and Pat. They are in the house. There is Lee. He is with his sister. He is with Pat. He is with his sister, Pat.

Pat is with Lee. Lee is Pat's brother. Pat is not playing. She is sitting. She is sitting down and looking at a book. It is a red book. Pat's book is red. Pat likes that book. That red book is very good. Pat likes to go in the house, sit down and look at her red book.

Lee is not sitting. He is not looking at his sister's red book. He is playing with a ball. That ball is red, too. Lee likes to play with his red ball. It is fun. He does not want to look at his sister's book. Lee does not like that book.

1. *Are Lee and Pat in the garden?*
2. *Where are they?*
3. *Is Pat sitting down?*
4. *What is she looking at?*
5. *Does Lee like Pat's book?*

New Words:	**her** (adj)
	now

Look at the children. Where are they now? They are in the garden. Now, Lee is playing with his sister in the garden. He is playing with his sister, Pat and his dog, Kim.

Now, Pat is playing with her brother. Pat likes her brother. She likes his dog, too. That dog likes to play. It likes to play with the children in the garden. It is playing with the children now.

Teacher 2
Where are the children now?

Daddy
They are in the garden.

Teacher 2
Is Lee with his sister?

Daddy
Yes, he is. He is with his sister, Pat.

Teacher 2

Is Kim there?

Daddy

Yes, he is. He is playing with the children.

Teacher 2

Does Kim like to play with the children?

Daddy

Yes, he does. He likes to play with the children in the garden.

Teacher 2

Is Pat playing with her brother?

Daddy

Yes, she is. She is playing with her brother and his dog in the garden.

Look at Lee. Lee is with his sister now. His sister's name is Pat. It is a good name, and Pat is a good girl. We like Pat, and we like her brother, too.

Now Pat is with her brother. Her brother's name is Lee. It is a good name. Lee likes his name and Pat likes her brother's name, too.

Pat's brother has a ball. He has a red ball. Lee likes to play with his red ball. He can play with his red ball in the garden. He is playing with his red ball now.

Lee's sister does not want to play with the ball now. She wants to look at her book. Pat really likes this book, and she is looking at it now.

1. *Is Lee with his sister?*
2. *What is his sister's name?*
3. *Do we like Lee and Pat?*
4. *Is Pat playing with the ball?*
5. *What is Pat looking at?*

5

New Words: **room**
                chair

Look at this room. This is the children's room. It is a very big room. This room is where the children can play. Lee and Pat like to play in this big room. It is fun.

Can you see the chairs in the room? The children can sit on the chairs. Lee can sit with Pat, and Pat can sit with Lee. They can sit on the chairs in the room and look at books.

Look at Lee and Pat. They are not looking at books now. They are playing. They are playing with the chairs. They are very happy. Lee is happy and his sister is happy, too. The children can have fun playing in this room.

Lee is playing with his sister in the big room. Where is Kim? Where is Kim, the dog? Kim is not here. Kim is not in the room with the children. Mommy does not want the dog to play in the children's room.

Mommy

Where is the dog? Where is Kim?

Pat

He's in the garden. The dog is in the garden, playing with the cat.

Mommy

Playing with the cat? Kim doesn't like the cat.

Pat

Kim doesn't want to be with the cat. He wants to be with us. He wants to be with Lee and me. He wants to come in this room and play with us.

Mommy

Kim can not come in this room. Daddy and I do not want the dog to come in the house now.

Pat

Kim is not happy, Mommy. He wants to come in the house. He wants to come in the house and play with us.

Now the cat and the dog are in the garden. The dog is not happy. The dog is not happy and the cat is not happy. The cat does not want to be with the dog. The cat does not want to play with the dog.

Cats do not like dogs, and dogs do not like cats. The dog and the cat want to go in the house. They want to go in the house and play with Lee and Pat. They want to play with Lee and Pat in the children's room.

Pat does not want to play with the cat now. She does not want to play with the cat, and she does not want to play with the dog. Pat wants to look at her book. She wants to look at her book, and she wants Lee to look at it, too.

Lee does not want to look at the book. He wants to go in the garden now. He wants to play in the garden. He wants to go in the garden and play with his ball. It is fun to play in the garden.

1. *Is the cat in the room now?*
2. *Where are the cat and the dog?*
3. *Does Pat want to play with the cat now?*
4. *What does Pat want to do?*
5. *Does Lee want to look at the book?*

6

New Words: **on**

Where are Lee and Pat now? Now, Lee and Pat are
at home. They are at home, with Mommy, Daddy and
their dog, Kim.

Pat is Lee's sister. Lee is with his sister now. Pat is
sitting on her chair. She is sitting on her chair and
looking at a book. Pat likes to do that.

Lee is not sitting on a chair. He is not looking at a
book. Lee does not want to look at a book. Lee wants
to play. Lee likes to play. He likes to play with his sister,
and he likes to play with Kim, too. He does not like to
play with the cat.

Lee does not like the cat. Now, Lee is playing with the
dog. He is playing with Kim. Lee and Kim are playing
with Lee's red ball.

Teacher 2
Where are Lee and Pat? Are they here?

Teacher 1
No, they are not.

Teacher 2
Where are they?

Teacher 1

They are at home.

Teacher 2

Lee and Pat are good children.

Teacher 1

Yes, they are. Lee is a good boy, and Pat is a very good girl.

Teacher 2

Pat is very good?

Teacher 1

Yes, she is. Pat likes to look at books. Pat likes to sit down and look at books.

Where is Pat now? Now, Pat is in her room. She is with her brother, Lee. Lee and Pat are sitting in the children's room. They are sitting on chairs. They are sitting on chairs and looking at a book.

That book is very good. Pat likes that book. She likes to look at that book, and she is looking at it now. Lee does not like that book. Lee does not want to look at books now

Lee does not like to sit down on chairs. He does not like to sit down on chairs and look at books. Lee wants to go in the garden. He wants to go and play in the garden. It is fun to play in the garden.

1. *Where is Pat now?*
2. *Is she with Lee?*
3. *Are Lee and Pat sitting down?*
4. *What are they sitting on?*
5. *Does Pat like to look at books?*

7

New Words: **table**
             give / giving

Now, Lee is in his room. He is sitting on his chair. He is sitting on his chair in the children's room. What is he looking at? Can you see what Lee is looking at?

Lee is looking at a book. The book is on a table. It is on a big table in the children's room. Lee likes this book. He does not like Pat's red book. He likes this book, and he likes to look at it.

Pat is in the room with Lee. She wants to look at the book, too. Pat likes books. Pat likes all books. Lee gives the book to his sister. Now Pat can look at the book, too.

Mommy

Do you want to look at this book, Pat?

Pat

Yes, I do. Can I? Can I look at that book?

Mommy

Yes, you can. I can give you the book. Here you are.

Pat

And can I sit here?

Mommy

Yes, you can. You can sit down on a chair at this table here. Do you want to look at the book now?

Pat

Yes, I do. Can you give me the book? Can you give me the book now?

Mommy

Yes, I can. Here you are. The book is on the table and you can look at it now.

Pat

Thank you. I like this book. I like all books. It's fun to look at books.

Mommy

Yes, it is. Now I can sit at the table and look at the book, too. I can look at the book with you. You can look at the book, and I can look at it, too.

Now Daddy is in the room, too. He is in the room with the children. Daddy has an ice cream. He has a very big ice-cream. Look at Daddy. Daddy is giving the big ice-cream to Pat.

Daddy gives the ice cream to Pat. Pat is very happy. Pat likes ice creams. All children like ice creams, don't they? Lee and Kim, the dog, are not happy. They are not happy with Daddy. Daddy does not have ice-creams to give to Lee and Kim.

1. *Does Pat like to look at books?*
2. *Where is Daddy?*
3. *What is Daddy giving Pat?*
4. *Is Pat very happy?*
5. *Do Lee and Kim have ice-creams?*

8

New Words: **new**
             for

Daddy has an ice-cream for Pat. He gives the ice-cream to Pat. Pat is very happy. She is happy with the ice-cream, and she is happy with Daddy, too.

Daddy does not have an ice-cream for Lee. He does not have an ice-cream for Lee, and he does not have an ice-cream for Kim, the dog. Lee and Kim are not happy. They are not happy with Daddy. They want to have ice-creams, too.

Pat is sitting down on a new chair. She is sitting on a new chair with her ice-cream. Lee and Kim are looking at Pat. They can see that she has an ice-cream. Lee and Kim are not happy. They are not happy with Pat. They can see she has an ice cream and they want to have ice-creams, too.

Lee
Is that ice-cream good?

Pat
Yes, it is. It is very good.

Lee
Can I have it? Can you give it to me?

Pat

No. No I can't. This ice-cream is not for you. This ice-cream is for me.

Lee

I don't like this. I am not happy. You have an ice-cream. I don't have an ice-cream.

Pat

Go and see Daddy. Daddy can give you an ice-cream, too.

Lee

No, he can't. Daddy likes you. He does not like me. He doesn't want to give me an ice-cream.

Pat

Yes, he does Lee. Daddy likes you and he wants to give you an ice-cream. Go on! Go and see Daddy.

Look at Daddy. Now, Daddy is giving Lee an ice-cream. He is giving Lee a big ice-cream. This big ice-cream is for Lee. Now, Lee has an ice-cream. He has a big ice-cream. Lee is happy now.

Lee and Pat like the ice-creams. Now, Pat has an ice-cream and Lee has an ice-cream, too. Kim does not have an ice-cream. Ice-creams are not for dogs, are they? Ice-creams are for children.

1. *Is Lee with his sister?*
2. *Does Pat have an ice-cream?*
3. *Can Daddy give Lee an ice-cream?*
4. *Does Kim, the dog, have an ice-cream?*
5. *Are ice-creams for dogs?*

9

New Words: **their**

Now, the children are in their room. They are in their room with Daddy. Lee is looking at Daddy. He can see Daddy has a chair. Daddy has a new chair for the children's room.

Daddy gives the new chair to Lee. Now, Lee can sit on his new chair. Pat wants a new chair, too. Now, Daddy is giving a new chair to Pat. Pat likes her new chair. Now, Lee and Pat are happy. They are happy with the new chairs for their room.

Teacher
Where are the children now?

Mommy
In their new room. The children are in their new room.

Teacher
Do they like their new room?

Mommy

Yes, they do. They have a table in their room and now they have chairs, too.

Teacher

Can Lee and Pat play in their new room?

Mommy

Yes, they can. They can play and they can look at books, too.

Teacher

Do Lee and Pat like to look at books?

Mommy

Pat does. Pat likes to look at books. Lee doesn't. Lee likes to play.

Teacher

Pat is a very good girl, isn't she?

Mommy

Yes, she is. She is a good girl. Lee is good, too. Pat is a good girl, and Lee is a good boy.

Mummy is in the house. She is at home. She is at home with her children. Mummy, Lee, Pat and their dog Kim are all in their house. They are in the children's room.

Mummy and the children are sitting down. They are sitting on their chairs. Mummy has a chair. Lee has a chair. Pat has a chair. Kim the dog does not have a chair. Chairs are not for dogs, are they?

1. *Are Lee, Pat and Mummy in their house?*
2. *Is Mummy with her children?*
3. *Do the children have new chairs for their room?*
4. *Can the children play in their room?*
5. *Does Pat like to look at books?*

10

New Words: **doing**
Who...?

Now, Lee is with his sister. He is with Pat. Lee and Pat are in their house. What are they doing? Can you see? They are playing. They are playing with Kim, the dog, in the children's room.

Lee is playing. Pat is playing. Kim, the dog is playing, too. They are all playing with Lee's big red ball. The children like to do that. They like to play with Kim and the big red ball.

Who is with the children now? Mummy is. Now, Mummy is in the room with the children. What is Mummy doing? Can you see? Can you see what Mummy is doing? Mummy is sitting on a chair and looking at her children. She likes to see the children play in their room.

Teacher 1

Where are the children now? Where are Lee and Pat?

Teacher 2

They are at home. They are in their house.

Teacher 1

What are they doing? Are they looking at books or are they playing?

Teacher 2

They are playing. They are playing with their dog in the children's room.

Teacher 1

Who is with the children? Is their daddy with the children?

Teacher 2

No, he is not. Their mummy is with the children.

Teacher 1

What is their mummy doing?

Teacher 2

She is sitting on a chair and looking at the children. She likes to see the children playing in their room.

Teacher 1

Is the children's dog in the children's room, too?

Teacher 2

Yes, he is. Kim, the dog, is playing with the children, too.

Who is this?
This is Lee. Lee is with his dog, Kim.

Who is that… over there?
That is Pat. Pat is over there with her mummy.

Who is this?
This is Daddy. Daddy is in the house. He is looking at a book.

Who are they?
They are Mummy, Daddy, Lee and Pat. Kim, the dog, is not here. Kim is playing in the garden.

1. Do Lee and Pat like to play with the dog?
2. Who is Lee's sister?
3. What are the children doing in the house?
4. Is Mummy with the children?
5. Does, Kim, the dog, like to play in the garden?

11

New Words: **Thank you**
               say / says

Lee is in his room with his sister, Pat. Pat is in the room with her brother, Lee. Kim, the dog, is in the room, too. They are all in the room.
What are they doing?
Can you see? Lee and Pat are looking at their Daddy.

What is Daddy doing? Can you see what Daddy is doing? Daddy is giving the children their new books. "The new books are for you," Daddy says. "Thank you," say the children. "Thank you for the new books."

Teacher 2
Who is Lee with now?

Teacher 1
He is with his sister, Pat. Lee is in his room with his sister.

Teacher 2
What are they doing?

Teacher 1

They are looking at their new books.

Teacher 2

New books? Do Lee and Pat have new books?

Teacher 1

Yes, they do.

Teacher 2

Do they like their new books?

Teacher 1

Yes, they do. They say their new books are very good.

Teacher 2

That is good. That is very good!

What is Mummy doing? Can you see? Can you see what Mummy is doing? Mummy is giving Lee an apple. "Here you are," says Mummy. Here is an apple for you." "Thank you," says Lee. "Thank you for this apple. I like it."

Now, Mummy is with Pat. She is giving Pat a banana and an orange. "Here you are Pat," she says. "This orange and this banana are for you.

"Thank you," says Pat. "Thank you for the orange and the banana. This orange looks very good. The banana looks very good, too. Thank you, Mummy."

1. What does Daddy give the children?
2. What does Mummy give Lee?
3. What does Mummy say to Lee?
4. What does Lee say to Mummy?
5. What does Pat say to Mummy?

12

New Words: **some**
             eat / eating

Now, the children are at home with Mommy and Daddy. Daddy has some apples to give to his children. The apples are on the table. They are on the table in the children's room.

What is Lee doing? Can you see? Lee is eating an apple. Lee likes to eat apples. "Thank you for the apples," Lee says.

Mommy has some ice-creams. She has some ice-creams to give to her children. Who is eating an ice-cream? Can you see? Pat is. Pat is eating an ice-cream. "Thank you for this ice-cream," Pat says. "It's very good!"

Teacher 1

Where are the children now? Are they at home?

Teacher 2

Yes, they are. They are at home with their mommy and daddy.

Teacher 1

What are they doing?

Teacher 2

They are eating.

Teacher 1

What are they eating?

Teacher 2

Lee is eating some apples, and Pat is eating an ice-cream.

Teacher 1

Does Lee like the apples? Does Pat like her ice-cream?

Teacher 2

Yes. Lee says the apples are very good, and Pat says her ice-cream is very good, too. The children are very happy now.

Teacher 1

That's good.

Teacher 2

Yes, it is. It's very good. I like to see happy children.

Where are the children? Can you see?
The children are in the house. They are at home. Pat is sitting down. She is sitting on a chair. Lee is not sitting down.

"Do you like the apples, Lee?" says Mommy. "Yes, I do," says Lee. "I like to eat apples. I like to eat bananas, too. I like to eat apples or bananas. I like to eat oranges, too."

"And ice-creams?" says Mommy. Do you like to eat ice-creams, too?" "Yes, I do," says Lee. I like to eat apples, bananas, oranges AND ice-creams.

Pat is looking at her brother. She is looking at Lee. She can see Lee has some apples. He has some bananas, some oranges and some ice creams, too. Pat says, "Lee likes to eat. He likes to eat apples. He likes to eat apples, bananas, oranges AND ice-creams!"

1. *Are the children in the garden?*
2. *Who are they with?*
3. *Who is giving some apples to the children?*
4. *Is Lee sitting down?*
5. *What does Lee like to eat?*

13

New Words: **today**
candy (sweets in British English)

Today, Lee and Pat are at home with their mommy. "Do you want an apple or a banana, Pat?" says Mommy. "An apple please," says Pat. "Please give me an apple. I like apples. Apples are good for us."

"Yes. Yes, they are," says Mommy. "Apples are good for us, and they are very good for children. Here you are. Here is an apple for you."

"Thank you," says Pat. Thank you for the apple." "What do you want to eat, Lee?" says Mommy. "I want some candy please," says Lee. Can I have some candy, please? Can you give me some candy, please?"

"No," says Mommy. "I do not want you to eat candy today. Please do not eat candy today. Candy is not good for you. Here you are. Here is an apple for you. Apples are good for you."

Teacher 2

Where are your children today? Where are Lee and Pat?

Daddy

They are at home. They are at home with their mommy.

Teacher 2

They are good children aren't they?

Daddy

Yes, they are. Lee is a good boy, and Pat is a very good girl.

Teacher 2

What do they like to eat? What do they eat at home?

Daddy

They like to eat what their mommy gives them. Today, their mommy is giving them some apples and some bananas.

Teacher 2

And candy? Is their mommy giving them candy today?

Daddy

No, she isn't. Their mommy says candy is not good for children.

Teacher 2

That's good. Candy is not very good for children. Apples and bananas are good for children. Candy is not.

Daddy

Lee is not very happy. Lee wants to have some candy today. Lee likes candy and he wants his mommy to give him some today.

What is this?

This is Lee's room. It is very big. It is a big room.
Today, the children can play in this room. They like
to play in this room. It is fun.

"Come here, Pat," says Lee. Come and play with me.
We can play at home today. Come and play with me
in my room."

"What do you have in your room?" says Pat. "I have
a ball," says Lee. I have a very big ball in my room.
We can play in my room with my big ball." And I
have some candy," says Lee. We can go in my room
and eat candy."

1. *Where are Lee and Pat today?*
2. *Is Pat a good girl?*
3. *Are apples good for children?*
4. *Can Mommy give Lee some candy today?*
5. *Does Lee have some candy in his room?*

14

New Words: **pen**
pencil

Today, Daddy is giving Lee a new pen. "This new pen is for you Lee," he says. "Thank you Daddy," says Lee. "Thank you for my new pen. I like it."

Daddy is giving Pat a pencil. He is giving her a new pencil. "This is for you Pat," he says. "This new pencil is for you." "Thank you for the pencil Daddy," says Pat.

Now Lee has a new pen. He has a pencil, too. His pen is new. His pencil is not new. Pat has a new pencil. She has a pen, too. Her pencil is new. Her pen is not new.

The children have new pens and pencils today. Lee has a new pen. He likes his new pen. Pat has a new pencil. She likes her new pencil. Lee and Pat are happy with their pens and pencils. They are happy with Daddy, too.

Teacher
Does Lee have a pen?

Mommy
Yes, he does. He has a new pen and he has some pencils, too.

Teacher
And Pat? Does Pat have a new pen, too?

Mommy

No she doesn't. Pat's pen is not new.

Teacher

Does she have some pencils?

Mommy

Yes, she does. Today she has a new pencil... a red pencil.

Teacher

Where are the children now?

Mommy

They are in their room.

Teacher

What are they doing in their room?

Mommy

Lee is playing with Kim, the dog. And Pat is looking at her books.

Now, the children have pens, pencils and books. Today, Lee does not want his pen. He gives his new pen to his sister. He gives it to Pat. "Here you are," he says. "Here is a new pen for you." "Thank you Lee," says Pat. "Thank you for the pen. I like this pen."

"I can give you my new pen," says Lee. "Can you give me some of your candy?" "Yes I can," says Pat. Here is some of my candy for you."

Pat gives some of her candy to her brother. Now, Lee is very happy. Pat has his new pen, and he has some of Pat's candy.

1. *Who gives Lee a new pen?*
2. *What does Daddy give to Pat?*
3. *Do the children like their pens and pencils?*
4. *Where are the children now?*
5. *Is Lee happy now?*

15

New Words: **walk / walking**

Today, Lee wants his books. He wants to look at his books in his room. He wants his pens and pencils, too. Now, he wants to go and see where his pens and pencils are.

"Excuse me," says Lee. "Excuse me, Daddy. Can you come into that room with me?" "Yes, I can," says Daddy. "What do you want to do in that room?" "I want to look for my books, pens and pencils," says Lee. "They are all in that room."

Lee and Daddy walk into the room. They walk into the room to look for Lee's books, pens and pencils.

Lee
Excuse me, Mommy.

Mommy
Yes, Lee. What do you want?

Lee
I want to go in the garden. Can I have some candy and go in the garden, please?

Mommy

What do you want to do in the garden?

Lee

I want to walk in the garden. I want to walk in the garden, eat some candy and look at the trees.

Mommy

Yes, Lee. You can have some candy and go and walk in the garden.

Lee

Thank you, Mommy.

Mommy

Here is some candy for you. This candy is for you and Pat.

Lee

Thank you, Mommy.

Mommy

The candy is for you AND your sister. Be a good boy and give some of the candy to your sister.

Now, Lee and Pat are walking in the garden. They are walking in the garden and looking at the trees. Kim, the dog, is walking with the children. Lee has some candy. He can give some of the candy to Pat. He can give some candy to Kim, too. Lee, Pat and Kim all like to eat candy.

"Let's go and sit down over there," says Lee. "let's sit down over there and eat the candy. This candy is very good." "Yes," says Pat. "Come on, Kim. Let's all sit down over there and eat some candy."

1. *What does Lee like to do in the garden?*
2. *Can Mommy give Lee some candy?*
3. *Is Kim, the dog, in the garden?*
4. *Does Kim like to eat candy?*
5. *Where can the children sit down?*

16

New Words: **school**
                road
                Excuse me

Now, the children are walking to school. Lee is walking to school and his sister, Pat, is walking to school too. They are on the road. This is a new road. It is not a road for cars. It is a road for children to walk to school on.

Kim, the dog, can walk to school too. He can walk on the new road with the children. He likes to do that. Kim likes to walk with Lee and Pat.

The children's school is not new. Lee and Pat do not want a new school. They like the school they have now. They like to go to this school. They like to walk there with their dog. They like to walk to school with Kim.

Teacher 2
Excuse me?

Daddy
Yes?

Teacher 2
Where are the children, now?

Daddy

They are going to school. They are walking to school with their dog, Kim.

Teacher 2

Is the dog going to school, too?

Daddy

Yes, it is. The dog is going to school with Lee and Pat

Teacher 2

Do the children have some candy today?

Daddy

No they don't.

Teacher 2

Can the children have candy when they are at school?

Daddy

No, they can not. Mommy and I do not want the children to eat candy when they are at school. They can eat apples, oranges and bananas. They can not eat candy at school.

Look at Lee and Pat. Lee and Pat are on the road with their dog, Kim. They are all walking to school. This road is for children to walk to school on. It is not a big road. It is a small road.

The road is small. It is a small road and it is very new. This road is only for children. It is not for cars. It is a road for children to walk to school on. Now, Lee and Pat are walking on the road. The children are walking on the road, and Kim the dog is walking with the children. They are all going to school.

1. *Where are the children going?*
2. *Is the dog with the children?*
3. *Do the children have some candy?*
4. *Are the children walking on the road?*
5. *Can cars go on this road?*

17

New Word: **old**

**Look over there.
Who can you see?**

We can see the children. We can see Lee and Pat. Lee and Pat are walking to school. We can see Kim, too. Kim, the dog, is walking with the children.

What can the children see?

The children can see a tree. This tree is very big. It is very big and it is very old. A cat is in the tree. That cat likes to go in trees, and it likes to go in this old tree. That cat is old, too. It is not like Pat's cat. Pat's cat is not old.

Lee and Pat can see the old cat. They can see the old cat in the tree. Kim, the dog, can see the old cat too. He is not happy. Kim does not like cats.

Mommy
Excuse me?

Teacher
Yes?

Mommy
What are the children doing now?

Teacher

They are walking to school. They are walking on the road.

Mommy

I am looking for a cat. It is an old cat. Is that old cat with the children?

Teacher

Yes, it is. That old cat is in an old tree. Lee and Pat are looking at the old cat now. Is that old cat very old?

Mommy

Yes, it is. That cat is very old. Pat's cat is not very old. That cat is very old.

Teacher

Do you like that old cat?

Mommy

Yes, I do. I like Pat's cat and I like that old cat, too.

Teacher

That cat is in a tree. The children are looking at that old cat now.

Is it a school?

Yes, it is. It is the children's school. It is not a big school. It is small. It is a small school. It is not a new school. It is old. It is an old school. The children do not want a new school. The children like their old school.

Who can you see over there?

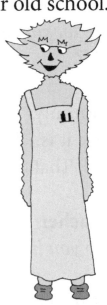

That is the teacher. She is the children's teacher. She is new. She is a new teacher. This new teacher is very good. Lee and Pat like this new teacher. Now, Lee and Pat are at the school. Now, they can go in the school with their new teacher.

1. *Can the children see an old tree?*
2. *What can they see in the tree?*
3. *Is Pat's cat old?*
4. *Does Kim like cats?*
5. *Do the children want a new school?*

18

New Words: **classroom**
together

Who is this? This is the teacher. The children have a new teacher today. The new teacher is in the classroom now. She is sitting on a chair and looking at a book.

Now, Lee and Pat want to go in the classroom. They want to go in together. They want to sit together in the classroom. The teacher can see Lee and Pat.

"Come on children," she says. "You can come in here. You can come in the classroom with us. Come in and sit down. We have some chairs for you. Come in and sit down. We can all sit together in this classroom."

"Please sit down here," says the new teacher. "Thank you," says Lee. "Thank you," says Pat. Now, all the children and the teacher are sitting down on their chairs in the classroom.

Daddy
Do the children have a new teacher today?

Mommy
Yes, they do.

Daddy
Where is the teacher now?

Mommy

She is in the classroom. She is in the classroom with the children.

Daddy

What are the children doing?

Mommy

They are looking at books. They are looking at books with their teacher.

Daddy

Are Lee and Pat sitting together?

Mommy

Yes, they are. Lee is sitting with Pat. Pat is sitting with Lee. Lee and Pat are sitting together with all the children in their classroom.

Daddy

That's good! And the teacher? Is the new teacher a good teacher?

Mommy

Yes, she is. This new teacher is very good.

Lee is sitting in the classroom with his sister, Pat. They are sitting together in the classroom. They are sitting together, and they are looking at the new teacher.

"The new teacher likes us," says Pat. "Yes, and we like the new teacher," says Lee. "It is good here," says Pat. It is good to be in this classroom with the new teacher. I like it."

Here is the new teacher with Lee and Pat. The children are giving the new teacher some apples to eat. "Thank you," says the teacher. "Thank you for the apples. I like apples. Let's sit down in the classroom and eat the apples together."

1. *Are Lee and Pat in their school?*
2. *Can they sit together in their classroom?*
3. *Is this teacher new?*
4. *Does the new teacher like Lee and Pat?*
5. *What do the children give their new teacher?*

19

New Words: **write**
               them

The teacher has some new books, pens and pencils for the children. She wants to give them to the children now. The teacher gives Lee a book. "This book is for you Lee," she says. "Thank you for the book," says Lee.

The teacher gives Pat a book. "This book is for you Pat," she says. "Thank you," says Pat. "Thank you for my new book." The teacher gives books to all the children in the classroom. She gives them all new books. These are books the children can write in.

Now, Lee and Pat have their new books. They want to write their names in their new books. They can do that. All the children in the classroom can write their names in their new books.

The teacher gives the children pens and pencils, too. She gives them pens and pencils. Now, the children can write with their pens and pencils. They want to write with them in their new books

Mommy
Excuse me!

Teacher
Yes?

Mommy
Do you have pens and pencils for the children?

Teacher

Yes, I do. I have pens and pencils for all the children. I have new books for them, too.

Mommy

That's good. Can the children write their names in their new books?

Teacher

Yes, they can. All the children can write their names in their new books.

Mommy

Do the children like their new books, pens and pencils?

Teacher

Yes, they do.

Mommy

That's good! Thank you for giving the children new books, pens and pencils.

Teacher

Thank you. I am happy to do that. I am happy to give them new books, pens and pencils.

"Please sit down," says the teacher. "Yes," Lee says to Pat. "Let's sit down here." The children sit down. They sit down on their chairs. All the children sit down, and Lee and Pat sit down together.

Lee sits down with his book and his new pen. Lee can write his name with his new pen. He can write his name in his new book. Today, Lee is good. Lee wants to be a good boy at school today.

Pat sits down at her table with her book and her pencil. She wants to write her name in her new book. She wants to write her name with her new pencil.

"Let's write," say Lee. "Yes," says Pat. "Let's write in the new books." Now, the teacher is looking at the children. She is looking at them write their names. She likes to see them do that. She likes to see them write in their books.

1. *Who has some books, pens and pencils for the children?*
2. *Does Pat have a new book?*
3. *Can the children write in their new books?*
4. *Where does Pat sit down?*
5. *What can Lee write with?*

20

New Words: **read / reading**
                well

Who is this? This is Lee. Lee is in the classroom. He is looking at the teacher. The classroom is new. It is not old. It is new. The children like to sit together in this new classroom.

Now, all the children are looking at the teacher. This teacher is new. She is a new teacher. All the children like this teacher. This teacher is very good to her children. This teacher likes to read to her children.

All the children and their teacher are together in the classroom. The children are sitting on their chairs and they are listening to the teacher. The teacher is reading them a book. This teacher likes to read to the children. This teacher reads very well and the children like it.

Daddy
Where are the children?

Mommy
They are at school. They are in their classroom with their new teacher.

Daddy
A new teacher? Is the new teacher good?

Mommy

Yes, she is. The new teacher is very good. This new teacher likes to read to the children. She likes to read to them in the classroom.

Daddy

That's good. Does the new teacher read well?

Mommy

Yes, she does. The new teacher reads very well.

Daddy

And Lee and Pat? Do they read very well, too?

Mommy

Not very well. The teacher reads very well. Lee and Pat do not read very well.

Daddy

I want Lee and Pat to read well.

Mommy

I want Lee and Pat to read well, too. At school, in their classroom, the teacher is reading to the children. The children like that. The children like the new teacher to read to them.

Look at the new teacher. The new teacher is in the classroom with the children. This new teacher can  read very well. She is good at reading. The children like this new teacher to read to them. The children like the new teacher to read to them, and the new teacher likes to read to the children.

The children are looking at their teacher. The teacher is reading to the children. She is reading them a new book. It is a very good book. All the children like this book.

Lee and Pat like this teacher. This teacher is very good to all the children in her classroom. She likes to see the children reading. She likes to see them writing, too. She likes to see them reading and writing.

1. *Where are the children?*
2. *Is the children's classroom new or old?*
3. *Do the children like this classroom?*
4. *Who can read very well?*
5. *Does the teacher like to see the children reading and writing?*

21

New Words: **put**
                your
                him

Now, all the children are in their classroom. Lee puts his book on the table and looks at it. He looks at his book. Lee likes this book. It is a very good book. It is not an old book. It is new. It is not a small book. It is big. Lee likes to read his big new book.

Pat puts her book on the table, too. Pat likes to read this book. It is not a very big book. It is small. It is not a new book. It is old. It is an old book. Pat likes to read her small old book.

Now, the teacher has some new books. She puts all the new books on her table. She puts the books on the table and the children can look at them there. Some of the books are big. Some of them are small. All the children want to look at the books. All the children want the teacher to give them a new book.

Now, the teacher is giving a book to Lee. She is giving his a new book. She wants Lee to read this book. She wants him to read well. She wants him to read the book to all the children in the classroom, and she wants him to read it well.

Teacher
Excuse me, children.

Children
Yes?

Teacher
Can you put all your books on my table, please?

Children

Yes, we can. Here you are. All the books are on your table now.

Teacher

Thank you. And please put your pens and pencils on my table, too. Put them with your books.

Children

There! All the books, pens and pencils are on your table now.

Teacher

Thank you. Now Lee, come here please. Children, look at Lee. Can you see him?

Children

Yes, we can. We can all see him.

Teacher

Good. Now, Lee is going to read to you. He is going to read his new book.

Children

Good! We want Lee to read to us. We want Lee to read his new book to us.

Now, Pat has a new writing book, too. This is a book for her to write in. It is not a reading book. It is a writing book. Pat puts her new writing book on the table. Pat likes to write in her new book. Pat can write very well now.

Lee has a new writing book, too. He is putting his new writing book on the table with Pat's book. Lee can write now. Lee can write in his writing book. Lee can write, but his sister Pat can write well. She can write VERY well.

The teacher is giving the children their writing books. She wants them to write their names in their new books. This teacher likes to see the children write. She likes to see them read, too. Now, all the children can read very well, and they can write very well, too.

1. *Where are the children now?*
2. *Does Pat like to read her book?*
3. *Who is giving books to the children?*
4. *What does the teacher want Lee to do?*
5. *Can Pat write very well now?*

22

New Words: **cold**
               hot

Now, Lee is writing in
his writing book. He is
writing, and the teacher
is looking at him write.
Pat is writing, too. She
is writing in her writing
book, too. The teacher
is looking at Lee and
Pat writing in their
writing books.

The teacher is looking at Lee's writing book. "Good!"
she says. You are a good boy. You can write very well
now." Now, the teacher is looking at Pat's writing book.
"Good, Pat!" she says. "You can write very well now,
and your brother can write very well, too."

The teacher is looking at the writing of all the children
in her classroom. "Good!" she says. "You are all good
children. You can all write very well now. Now, please
put your pens down. Put them down on the table with
your writing books."

Mommy
Where is Pat now? What is she doing?

Daddy
She's in her classroom. She's giving her writing book to her teacher.

Mommy
What does the teacher say to Pat?

Daddy

She says, "Good, Pat! You are a good girl. You can write very well, now."

Mommy

And Lee's writing? Does the teacher look at Lee's writing, too?

Daddy

Yes, she does. She says Lee can write very well now, too.

Mommy

This teacher is very good, isn't she?

Daddy

Yes, she is. She likes all the children in her classroom, and she likes to see them all reading and writing.

Mommy

I'm very happy that Lee and Pat have a good teacher.

Daddy

I am happy, too. I'm happy they have a good teacher and a good school.

Today, it is cold in the children's classroom. It is not hot. It is cold. It is very cold. Pat is cold. Lee is cold, and the teacher is cold, too. They are all cold.

The children do not want to write now. They do not want to write, and they do not want to sit in their classroom and read their books. They do not want to be in the classroom. They want to go in the garden and play.

The school has a big garden. Lee, Pat and all the other children can play together in the school garden. The children do not want to be cold. They do not like to be cold. They want to go and play together in the school garden.

1. *Does the teacher say Pat can write very well, now?*

2. *Is this new teacher very good?*

3. *Are Mommy and Daddy happy?*

4. *Is it hot today?*

5. *Where can the children play?*

23

New Word: **game**

Now, Lee and Pat are not sitting in the classroom. They are not reading or writing. **Where are they? What are they doing?** They are in the school garden, and they are playing. They are playing a game. They are playing a game with their ball in the school garden.

Look at the children. Look at Lee and Pat. Now, the children are not cold. They are playing a game in the garden and they are not cold now. The teacher is looking at the children. She likes to see them play games in the school garden. She wants the children to be happy. She says it is good for children to play games together.

Now the children are not cold and the teacher wants the children to go into the classroom. "Please put down the balls and go into the classroom," she says. "Please go in the classroom, sit down and look at your books."

Boy
Excuse me?

Pat
Yes? What do you want?

Boy
Is this your ball?

Pat

No, it isn't. It's Lee's ball.

Boy

Where is your ball?

Pat

I don't have a ball. I play with Lee's ball. Lee is my brother.

Boy

Can we play with your brother's ball now?

Pat

No, we can't. The teacher wants us to go in the classroom now.

Boy

It's cold in the classroom. I want to be in the garden. I want to play in the garden.

Pat

We can't play in the garden now. The teacher wants us to go in the classroom. She wants us to go in the classroom, sit down and look at our books.

Now, all the children are in the classroom. They are not looking at their books now. They are eating. Lee has an apple. He has some water, too. Pat wants to have some water. She is hot and she wants to have some cold water.

"Can I have you water, please?" says Pat. "Yes, you can," says Lee. "Here you are." Lee gives his water to Pat. The water is not hot. It is cold. It is very cold. The children are hot now, and they want the water to be cold. Lee and Pat like cold water.

1. *Is it hot in the classroom today, or is it cold?*
2. *Do Lee and Pat like to play in the school garden?*
3. *What does the teacher like to see?*
4. *What is Lee eating?*
5. *Can Lee give his sister some water?*

24

New Words: **friend**
                black

Today, Pat is sitting in the classroom. She is sitting with her new friend. Pat and her friend like to sit together in the classroom. Pat's friend has a new pen. This new pen is black. Pat's friend likes her new, black pen.

"Can you give me your black pen?" says Pat. "Yes, I can," says Pat's friend. "What do you want it for?" "I want to write your name," says Pat. "I want to write your name here in this book. This is my writing book." "Here you are," says Pat's friend. Here is a black pen for you to write with."

Mommy
Who is Pat sitting with?

Teacher 2
Her friend. Pat is sitting with her friend.

Mommy
Do Pat and her friend have books, pens and pencils?

Teacher 2
Yes, they do. Now, Pat is writing with her friend's black pen.

Mommy
Can Pat write well now?

Teacher 2
Yes, she can. Pat can write well now, and she likes to write in her writing book.

Mommy
Can Pat's friend write well, too?

Teacher 2
Yes, she can. Pat's friend can write very well now.

Mommy
That's good! I want the children to write well. I want them to read well, too.

Teacher 2
Pat and her friend can read and write well now. Lee and his friends can write well now, too. Now, all the children can read and write very well.

Now, Lee and Pat are not in the classroom. They are in the garden. They are in the garden with Kim, the dog. Pat's new friend is in the garden, too. Pat's new friend likes Kim. She wants to play with Kim. She wants to play with Kim in the school garden.

"I like your dog," says Pat's new friend.
"Do you?" says Pat. "Yes, I do," says Pat's friend.
"Your dog is very good. It likes to play games. It likes to play games, and it is very good with children. What is your dog's name?"

"Kim," says Pat. "Our dog's name is Kim. "That is a very good name," says Pat's friend. I like your dog. I like your dog's name. I like you, and I like your brother Lee, too."

1. *Does Pat have a new friend?*
2. *What does Pat want to do with her friend's pen?*
3. *Can Pat write well now?*
4. *Where does Pat's friend want to play with the dog?*
5. *What is the dog's name?*

25

New Words: **a lot (of)**

Today, a lot of the children are playing a game in the classroom. Pat is playing with her brother and with her friends. The children are not playing in the road or in the garden. They are playing in the school.

Look at the game. Can you see it? A lot of the children like this game. Kim, the dog, can see the game. He wants to play the game. He wants to play this game with the children. Can he? Can Kim play the game with the children? "Come on, Kim," says Lee. "Come and play. Come and play this game with us."

Now, Kim is playing. He is playing the game with the children. This dog likes to play games. Kim likes children, and he likes to play games with children. Kim is very good at playing games. He is very good at playing games with children.

Mommy
Can the children play in school today?

Teacher 2
Yes, they can. Today, the children can play in the classroom. They are playing now.

Mommy
Who is Pat playing with?

158

Teacher 2

She is playing with a lot of her friends and with Kim the dog.

Mommy

Kim is playing in the classroom, too?

Teacher 2

Yes, he is. Kim likes to play with the children. This dog likes to play games.

Mommy

Kim likes to play games at home, too. He is very good at playing games. He is very good at playing with the children.

Teacher 2

Yes, I can see that. Kim is a very good dog. I like dogs that like to play with children.

Mommy

Kim likes to play with children. He does not like to play with cats. Kim does not like cats.

The children are not playing now. They are sitting down in their classroom and they are writing in their books. Today, it is hot in the classroom. It is very hot. The children are hot, and the teacher is hot, too.

The teacher wants to look at the children's writing. She says, "Pat. Please come here. I want to look at your writing book. Please come here and give me your writing book."

Pat goes to the teacher and puts her writing book on her table. The teacher looks at it. "Good!" she says. "Your writing is very good today. You can write very well now. You are a good girl. Your brother is good, too. Your brother is a good boy and your dog, Kim, is very, very good!"

1. *Where can the children play today?*
2. *Is Kim good at playing games?*
3. *Who can Pat play with?*
4. *Does the teacher like Kim?*
5. *Can Pat write very well, now?*

26

New Words: **take**
from

Look here. Is this Mommy or Daddy? This is Mommy. Today, Mommy is going from the house. She is going to the school. She is going to take the children home from school. The children want to go home now. They can go home from school with Mommy in the car.

Where is Mommy now? Can you see her? Mommy is coming down the road in her car. She is coming to the school. She is coming to take Lee and Pat home from school.

Look at the car on the road. Mommy does not have a new car. Her car is old. Mommy's car is very old. Lee and Pat like this old car. They like it a lot. "We like your car," they say. "We like your old, black car. We want to go home with you in the old, black car."

Teacher 1

What is Pat's mommy doing now? Where is she?

Teacher 2

She is on the road. She is on the road in her car. She is coming to take Lee and Pat home from school.

Teacher 1

Do the children want to go home now?

Teacher 2

Yes, they do. All the children want to go home now, and Lee and Pat want to go home in the car with their mommy. They like that car.

Teacher 1

Is their car new or is it old?

Teacher 2

It is old. It is very old. Lee and Pat like their mommy's old car.

Teacher 1

Don't they want a new car?

Teacher 2

No they don't. They like their old car. They like that car a lot.

Teacher 1

And you? Is your car new or old?

Teacher 2

I don't have a car. The children's mommies and daddies have cars. I don't have a car.

Here is Mommy in her car. She is on the road in her old, black car. She is coming to take Lee and Pat home from school. The children like to go home in Mommy's car. Today, they do not want to walk home. They want to go home in the car with their mommy. They like to go in this car.

Today, Pat's friend wants to go in the car, too. She wants to go to Pat's house with Pat. Pat likes her friend, and she wants her to see her house. Pat's friend can go in the car with Pat and Lee. They can all go home from school together.

And Kim, the dog? Kim wants to go home, too. Can he? Can Kim go home in the car with Mommy and the children? Yes, he can. Kim can go home with Mommy, Lee, Pat and Pat's friend. All of them can go home together. All of them can go home in Mommy's old, black car.

1. *Where is Mommy going?*
2. *Who is she going to see?*
3. *Can the children go home in the car?*
4. *Is the car new or old?*
5. *Who wants to go home with Pat?*

27

New Words: **every**
              day

Lee and Pat are going to Mommy's car. They are going home. They are going home with Mommy, Pat's friend and Kim, the dog. Mommy is taking them home from school. Mommy likes to do this. She does this every day when the children are at school. "Let's go home," says Mommy. "Yes. Let's go home," say the children.

The children like to go in Mommy's car. They like Mommy's car a lot and they want to go in the car every day. "Come on, children," says Mommy. "Put your books in the car. Let's go home."

The children put their books in the car and sit down in the car. Now, they can all go home. Mommy can take them all home from school. She can take them all home in her car.

Teacher 1

Where are the children going now?

Teacher 2

They are all going home from school. All the children are going home and Lee and Pat are going home in their mommy's car.

Teacher 1

And their dog, Kim? Are they taking Kim home, too?

Teacher 2
Yes, they are. Their mommy is taking Kim home in the car, too.

Teacher 1
Does Kim like to be in the car?

Teacher 2
Yes, he does. Kim likes to be in the car with the children. He likes to be at home, and he likes to be with the children at school, too.

Teacher 1
Does Kim come to school with Lee and Pat every day?

Teacher 2
Yes, he does. He likes to come to school. He comes to school with Lee and Pat every day.

Teacher 1
Kim is a very good dog, isn't he?

Teacher 2
Yes, he is. He is a very good dog. I like Kim. I like him a lot.

Lee and Pat are going to Mommy's car. They are going home. They are going home with Mommy, Pat's friend and Kim, the dog. Mommy is taking them home from school. Mommy likes to do this. She does this every day when the children are at school. "Let's go home," says Mommy. "Yes. Let's go home," say the children.

The children like to go in Mommy's car. They like Mommy's car a lot and they want to go in the car every day. "Come on, children," says Mommy. "Put your books in the car. Let's go home."

The children put their books in the car and sit down in the car. Now, they can all go home. Mommy can take them all home from school. She can take them all home in her car.

1. *Where are Lee and Pat going?*
2. *Who are they going with?*
3. *Do the children want to go in Mommy's car every day?*
4. *Can Mommy take them all in her car?*
5. *Where does Kim like to go?*

The End

Thank you for making it to the end of our book. To continue learning with Word by Word Graded Readers, please move on to the next book - **Book 5: 'Lee has a friend'**

http://hyperurl.co/0v5r4j

To see the full range of Word by Word graded readers for children and access our notes for teachers and parents, please visit our website at:

http://wordbywordseries.com/